Team Spirit

THE CHICAGO CUBS

BY

MARK STEWART

Content Consultant
James L. Gates, Jr.
Library Director
National Baseball Hall of Fame and Museum

NORWOOD HOUSE PRESS

CHICAGO, ILLINOIS

Norwood House Press
P.O. Box 316598
Chicago, Illinois 60631

For information regarding Norwood House Press, please visit our website at:
www.norwoodhousepress.com or call 866-565-2900.

All photos courtesy of AP/Wide World Photos, Inc. except the following:
Old Judge & Gypsy Queen (6 top); Author's Collection (6 bottom, 7, 19, 34 top, 37);
Bowman Gum Co. (14, 35 left); Spaulding & Merrick Co. (16); Sweet Caporal (16,17);
Turkey Red (17); Ramly Co. (18); Topps, Inc. (20, 35 right & bottom, 40 bottom);
Allen & Ginter (34 left); Little Recruit (34 right); John Klein (38, 39);
Exhibit Supply Co. (40 top); Goudey Gum Co. (41 bottom).
Special thanks to Topps, Inc.

Editor: Mike Kennedy
Designer: Ron Jaffe
Consulting Editor: Steve Krasner
Project Management: Black Book Partners, LLC.

Special thanks to Sandy Brogmus

Library of Congress Cataloging-in-Publication Data

Stewart, Mark, 1960-
  The Chicago Cubs / by Mark Stewart ; with content consultant James L.
Gates,Jr.
    p. cm. -- (Team spirit)
  Summary: "Presents the history, accomplishments and key personalities
of the Chicago Cubs baseball team. Includes timelines, quotes, maps,
glossary and websites"--Provided by publisher.
  Includes bibliographical references and index.
  ISBN-13: 978-1-59953-001-7 (library edition : alk. paper)
  ISBN-10: 1-59953-001-5 (library edition : alk. paper)
  1. Chicago Cubs (Baseball team)--History--Juvenile literature. I.
Gates,Jr.,James L. II. Title. III. Series.
  GV875.C6S84 2006
  796.357'640977311--dc22
                                                            2005033539

COVER PHOTO: Jeromy Burnitz gets high fives from his teammates
after belting a home run in 2005.

Table of Contents

SPORTS WORDS & VOCABULARY WORDS: In this book, you will find many words that are new to you. You may also see familiar words used in new ways. The glossary on page 46 gives the meanings of baseball words, as well as "everyday" words that have special baseball meanings. These words appear in **bold type** throughout the book. The glossary on page 47 gives the meanings of vocabulary words that are not related to baseball. They appear in ***bold italic type*** throughout the book.

Meet the Cubs

Imagine what it might be like to have a professional baseball team in your own neighborhood. Think of how much fun it would be if everyone—from the players to the peanut vendors—was someone who lived around the corner or down the street. That is the way Chicago feels about the Cubs.

The Cubs have played in the same *quaint* neighborhood ballpark on the city's north side for more than 90 years. The world outside has changed tremendously, but inside Wrigley Field's ivy-covered walls, time seems to slow down. It is a place where the players and the fans are comfortable being themselves. It is a place where legends are born and heroes are made.

This book tells the story of the Cubs, who have played in the same city longer than any team in American sports. The spirit of the Chicago players can be seen every time they take the field. Being a Cub is about more than winning and losing. It means playing hard and caring deeply for the game of baseball.

Mark Prior and Todd Walker show the team spirit that makes the Cubs one of the most enjoyable teams to watch.

Way Back When

The Cubs have played in Chicago since 1874. No sports team in the United States has represented its city longer. The team was called the White Stockings during the 1870s and 1880s. This club was one of the best in the **National League (N.L.)**. The White Stockings won the **pennant** in 1876, and five times between 1880 and 1886. The star of the team was Cap Anson. He was one of the league's best hitters and the team's manager for many years. He led the N.L. in **runs batted in (RBIs)** eight times.

After Anson retired, the Cubs rebuilt their team and won the pennant each season from 1906 to 1908, and again in 1910. The heart of this club was its great infield of Frank Chance,

TOP: Cap Anson, a strong hitter and smart manager.
LEFT: The great Cubs team that won four pennants in five seasons. Frank Chance is front and center.

HEY! WATCH where you're driving, Lead-Foot!!!

Hi, FLIPPY. What'cha doing?

The End.

'cuz he's a **Jerk!**

Why?

…o from the 1930s. Hack Wilson is in the center, …bby Hartnett is on the far right.

…and Harry Steinfeldt. The Cubs also had an …hich was led by Ed Reulbach and Mordecai …o of Brown's fingers had been *mangled* in …nusual grip made his pitches dart suddenly

…the Cubs had some very good teams and …hey won four pennants between 1929 …the N.L.'s best teams every year during …arred Hack Wilson, Gabby Hartnett, …ot, Kiki Cuyler, Riggs Stephenson, Lon …Stan Hack—all of whom were among

In 1945, the Cubs beat the St. Louis Cardinals for the N.L. pennant. It was their 10th league title in less than 50 years. The Cubs then lost a thrilling **World Series** to the Detroit Tigers. Though Chicago fans were disappointed, they could hardly wait for the team's next trip to the World Series. It turned out to be a long wait.

Over the next 60 seasons, the Cubs failed to win another pennant. They came close many times, but some bit of bad luck always seemed to strike. Great players like Hank Sauer, Ernie Banks, Ron Santo, Billy Williams, Fergie Jenkins, Bruce Sutter, Andre Dawson, Ryne Sandberg, Mark Grace, Greg Maddux, and Sammy Sosa wore the Chicago uniform during this time. Sauer, Banks, Dawson, Sandberg, and Sosa won the **Most Valuable Player (MVP)** award, but none was able to lead the Cubs back to the World Series.

Some fans believe it was more than bad luck that kept the Cubs from winning another pennant. They say that the team was cursed. Could it be true? It is just one of many fascinating stories about this beloved team.

LEFT: Ernie Banks, the team's greatest player. He was the National League MVP in 1958 and 1959. **TOP:** Ryne Sandberg, Chicago's slugging second baseman. He won the MVP award in 1984.

The Team Today

Chicago is an *earnest*, hard-working city. Chicago fans demand nothing less from their Cubs. The team tries to find players who perform like stars but who do not behave like big shots. This is especially true when it comes to pitching.

The Cubs have had some very good pitchers in recent years. However, if you met them on the street or saw them in a restaurant, you would never know from the way they acted that they are celebrities. When you see Chicago pitchers on the mound, however, they are all business.

On the other hand, Chicago hitters are all smiles. They love hitting in their home park. When the sun warms the field and a breeze makes the flags dance, the outfield walls of Wrigley Field seem so close that batters can reach out and grab a handful of ivy.

Naturally, the Cubs like to have powerful hitters—and powerful hitters like to play for the Cubs. Hitting a home run in the **major leagues** is never easy, but when you hit one out of Wrigley Field, it often sails over the bleachers and into the street.

Aramis Ramirez greets Derrek Lee after a home run.
The two sluggers continued the team's tradition of power hitting.

11

Home Turf

Wrigley Field is one of baseball's most beautiful ballparks. It was built in 1914 and originally called Weeghman Park. Almost all of the seats are in the **grandstand** area, and fans sit very close to the players and the field. Unlike other stadiums, the **bleacher seats** are the most popular. More than one Cubs fan has said that you cannot truly know Chicago until you have spent an afternoon among the "bleacher bums" of Wrigley Field.

Wrigley Field is rich in *tradition*. The ivy growing on the outfield walls was planted in 1937. The old-time scoreboard also dates back to 1937. From 1914 to 1987, only day games were played. Lights were added in 1988, but the Cubs still play more day games than any other team. Wrigley Field's most famous tradition happens when an opponent hits a home run. The fans never keep the ball as a *souvenir*—they always throw it back.

WRIGLEY FIELD BY THE NUMBERS

- *There are 39,538 seats in Wrigley Field.*
- *The distance from home plate to the left field foul pole is 355 feet.*
- *The distance from home plate to the center field fence is 400 feet.*
- *The distance from home plate to the right field foul pole is 353 feet.*

The fans enjoy another beautiful afternoon at Wrigley Field.
INSET: Sammy Sosa jumps into the ivy in an attempt to catch a fly ball.

Dressed for Success

The Cubs have worn more that 30 different uniforms over the last 135 years. Almost every one has featured some combination of white and blue. The team has not been afraid to experiment. The Cubs were the first to try sleeveless uniforms, and the first to try a uniform color that matched the animal they were named after. The little cub first appeared on Chicago uniforms in 1908. Since World War I, the Cubs have tried to use red along with their traditional white and blue.

In recent years, the Cubs have worn a number of uniforms that remind fans of their old styles. This has made souvenir collectors very happy, because there is almost always something new to buy. Chicago fans especially like the blue caps with the red visors—something the team had never tried before.

Pitcher Bob Rush models the Cubs uniform of the early 1950s.

UNIFORM BASICS

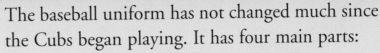

The baseball uniform has not changed much since the Cubs began playing. It has four main parts:

- a cap or batting helmet with a sun visor;
- a top with a player's number on the back;
- pants that reach down between the ankle and the knee;
- stirrup-style socks.

The uniform top sometimes has a player's name on the back. The team's name, city, or *logo* is usually on the front. Baseball teams wear light-colored uniforms when they play at home, and darker styles when they play on the road.

For more than 100 years, baseball uniforms were made of wool *flannel* and were very baggy. This helped the sweat *evaporate* and gave players the freedom to move around. Today's uniforms are made of *synthetic* fabrics that stretch with players and keep them dry and cool.

Mark Prior wears the Cubs' gray road uniform.

We Won!

The Cubs have had some amazing victories during their long history. Their most famous came in 1908, at the Polo Grounds in New York. The Cubs had won the World Series the previous fall, and were trying to become the first team to win it twice in a row. The New York Giants were the only team good enough to stop them.

In a September game between the two teams, New York's Al Bridwell broke a 1–1 tie in the bottom of the ninth inning with a single. At least, that is what the fans thought. The runner on first base, Fred Merkle, did

LEFT: Johnny Evers, one of the craftiest players of his day.   **ABOVE**: Al Bridwell, whose single should have won the game for the Giants.

RIGHT: Fred Merkle, whose base-running blunder gave the Cubs a chance to win the pennant. **BELOW**: Ray Kroh, who found the missing baseball.

not bother to touch second base once the winning run had scored, and headed for the Giants' clubhouse.

Second baseman Johnny Evers saw that Merkle had failed to touch second. He knew if he could get the ball and touch the base, it would be a **force-out**. The winning run would not count. The only problem was that the crowd had swarmed all over the field, and the ball was loose among the fans. Shortstop Joe Tinker managed to find the ball, but New York's first base coach snatched it from him and threw it into the stands!

Ray Kroh, a pitcher on the Cubs, found the fan who caught the ball and demanded it back. When the fan refused, Kroh punched him in the nose and took the ball. He handed it to Evers, who made sure umpire Hank O'Day was nearby. When Evers stepped on the base, O'Day stuck his thumb in the air. "Out!" he cried. The league ruled that the game had to be replayed—if necessary.

As luck would have it, the Giants and Cubs finished the season with *identical* records of 98–55. They met again in New York to replay the game. The Giants took an early lead, but the Cubs came back against New York's great pitcher, Christy Mathewson. Mordecai Brown pitched well in **relief**, and Chicago hung on to win 4–2.

Mordecai Brown

Two days later, the Cubs took the field against the Detroit Tigers in the first game of the World Series. If the Chicago pitchers could not stop the great Ty Cobb and his teammates, their marvelous victory would be forgotten. Once again, Brown was the hero. He won Game One as a relief pitcher, then shutout the Tigers in Game Four. Orval Overall

A scorecard from the 1908 World Series,
with a cartoon of Detroit star Ty Cobb.

also won two games. The Cubs won the series four games to one, and limited the Tigers to a .203 batting average.

This same Chicago ball club won the pennant in 1910, but lost to Philadelphia Athletics. The Cubs returned to the World Series six more times, but failed to win it all again. The fans who celebrated their team's victory in 1908 never imagined that they would not win again during the 20th century.

Go-To Guys

To be a true star in baseball, you need more than a quick bat and a strong arm. You have to be a "go-to guy"—someone the manager wants on the pitcher's mound or in the batter's box when it matters most. Cubs fans have had a lot to cheer about over the years, including these great stars…

THE PIONEERS

CAP ANSON   First Baseman

• BORN: 4/17/1852   • DIED: 4/14/1922   • PLAYED FOR TEAM: 1876 TO 1897

Adrian "Cap" Anson was the most important person in baseball during the 1800s. He was a powerful hitter and a good manager who played for Chicago until he was 45 years old. When Anson retired, the team changed its name to Orphans for many years because they had lost their "father."

GABBY HARTNETT   Catcher

• BORN: 12/20/1900   • DIED: 12/20/1972   • PLAYED FOR TEAM: 1922 TO 1940

Gabby Hartnett was baseball's first power-hitting catcher. He was behind the plate for four pennant winners, and was the N.L. MVP in 1935.

ERNIE BANKS   Shortstop/First Baseman

• BORN: 1/31/1931   • PLAYED FOR TEAM: 1953 TO 1971

Ernie Banks was nicknamed "Mr. Cub." His love of baseball made fans forget that the Cubs were not a very good team while he played for them. Banks hit 512 home runs and was named N.L. MVP in 1958 and 1959.

Ernie Banks   1ST BASE

BILLY WILLIAMS   Outfielder

• BORN: 6/15/1938   • PLAYED FOR TEAM: 1959 TO 1974

When Billy Williams was on a hot streak, no hitter in baseball was more dangerous. He once went eight-for-eight in a **doubleheader**, and he won the league batting championship in 1972. Between 1963 and 1970, Williams played in 1,117 games in a row.

FERGIE JENKINS   Pitcher

• BORN: 12/13/1942   • PLAYED FOR TEAM: 1966 TO 1973, 1982 TO 1983

Fergie Jenkins was one of the best pitchers in baseball when he played for the Cubs. He had a great fastball, and a good **slider**, too. Jenkins won 20 or more games six seasons in a row for the Cubs.

RON SANTO   Third Baseman

• BORN: 2/25/1940   • PLAYED FOR TEAM: 1960 TO 1973

Ron Santo was the N.L.'s best **all-around** third baseman during the 1960s. He was a powerful hitter, a slick fielder, and a *fiery* leader. Santo later announced Cubs games on television and radio.

RON SANTO   3rd base

TOP: Ernie Banks   **RIGHT**: Ron Santo

MODERN STARS

RYNE SANDBERG   Second Baseman

• Born: 9/18/1959   • Played for Team: 1982 to 1997

Ryne Sandberg led the Cubs to the **postseason** for the first time in almost 40 years in 1984. He was voted the N.L. MVP that season.

MARK GRACE   First Baseman

• Born: 6/28/1964   • Played for Team: 1988 to 2000

Mark Grace had more hits than any player in baseball during the 1990s. He was also one of the Cubs fans' favorite players.

SAMMY SOSA   Outfielder

• Born: 11/12/1968   • Played for Team: 1992 to 2004

Sammy Sosa was the greatest power hitter in team history. He slugged 60 or more home runs three times, and had more than 100 RBIs nine years in a row.

KERRY WOOD   Pitcher

• Born: 6/16/1977   • First Year with Team: 1998

Kerry Wood used his blazing fastball and hard-breaking curve to become one of the best pitchers in team history. He was the N.L. **Rookie of the Year** in 1998.

CARLOS ZAMBRANO   Pitcher

- BORN: 6/1/1981   • FIRST YEAR WITH TEAM: 2001

Carlos Zambrano reminded fans of old-time pitchers when he joined the team The hard-throwing, emotional Venezuelan wanted to pitch nine innings every time he started a game.

MARK PRIOR   Pitcher

- BORN: 9/7/1980   • FIRST YEAR WITH TEAM: 2002

The Cubs chose Mark Prior with the second pick in the 2001 **draft**. He pitched in just nine **minor league** games before joining the Chicago pitching staff, then became one of the best pitchers in baseball.

DERREK LEE   First Baseman

- BORN: 9/6/1975
- FIRST YEAR WITH TEAM: 2004

Derrek Lee learned how to play baseball in Japan, where his father was a star in the 1970s and 1980s. The graceful fielder and powerful hitter became an **All-Star** after he joined the Cubs.

LEFT: Sammy Sosa
RIGHT: Derrek Lee

On the Sidelines

In baseball's early days, it was not unusual for a team's best player to be its manager, too. Sometimes this worked out, and sometimes it did not. When the Cubs had "player-managers," good things usually happened.

From 1876 to 1910, Al Spalding, Cap Anson, and Frank Chance won eight pennants for the team. In 1932, first baseman Charlie Grimm took over the after 99 games and led the Cubs to another pennant. Grimm stepped aside in 1938 and catcher Gabby Hartnett became the manager. Guess what? He guided the Cubs to the pennant that year, too!

One of the most beloved Cubs never played or managed a game for the team. His name was Harry Caray and he was part of Cubs baseball for more than 15 seasons. Caray broadcast the team's games on television and radio and was a friend to fans and players alike. He was famous for leading the crowd in song during the seventh-inning stretch.

Harry Caray likes the look of this larger-than-life cartoon of himself.

One Great Day

Everybody who had seen Kerry Wood pitch in the minor leagues predicted he would make a good major leaguer. But no one knew that he would be so good—so soon. When Wood walked to the mound on a gray afternoon to face the Houston Astros, it was only his fifth start as a member of the Cubs.

Wood had his "good stuff" that day. His fastball was hissing across home plate at almost 100 miles per hour. His curve was bending sharply just as batters started their swings. The first five Astros were helpless against Wood. Each struck out. The next six batters had more luck. They all hit the ball, and one reached first base on a slow grounder. This would be the only hit for the Astros all day.

Wood struck out the next five batters. Each watched strike three sizzle into the catcher's mitt. They knew they had no chance to hit Wood's pitches, so they did not even try. Wood **struck out the side** in the seventh and eighth innings, giving him 18 strikeouts for the game. He needed two more to match the record for the most strikeouts in a nine-inning game. The record was held by his boyhood hero, Roger Clemens.

First baseman Mark Grace embraces Kerry Wood and catcher Sandy Martinez gives him a pat on the back after his 20th strikeout.

In the ninth inning, Wood struck out the **leadoff hitter**, Bill Spiers, and then Craig Biggio grounded out. The final batter, Derek Bell, swung and whiffed at three hard-breaking sliders—the last one he missed by more than a foot. The Cubs won 2–0. The hat Wood wore that day now is on display in the **Hall of Fame**, but the 20th strikeout ball is not. Wood gave it to his mom.

Legend Has It

Cap Anson

Did Cap Anson save baseball in the 1880s?

LEGEND HAS IT that he did. In the early days of the National League, many teams were having money troubles. Anson used good, young players to build Chicago into a mighty team. He became America's most famous player. Fans around the league streamed into the ballpark when Anson and his stars came to town. Anson understood the future of baseball when others did not. Sadly, he did not see a place in the game for African-Americans. Anson used his power to keep them from playing in the big leagues.

Who hit the longest home run in the history of Wrigley Field?

LEGEND HAS IT that it was Dave Kingman. The 6' 7" slugger played for the Cubs from 1978 to 1980, but it was as a member of the New York Mets that he made history on a windy day in 1976. Kingman drove a pitch to left-center field that went over the fence, out of the stadium, over Waveland Avenue, and four houses up Kenmore Avenue. The ball crashed into a third-story porch 550 feet from home plate!

Were the Cubs "cursed" in 1945?

LEGEND HAS IT that they were. Mike Sianis, who owned a nearby *tavern*, bought two tickets to Game Four of the 1945 World Series and brought his billy goat, Murphy, for good luck. At first, the ushers let him in. But when other fans complained about the smell, the Cubs' owner ordered him to leave. Sianis was so angry that he put a curse on the team. He said they would never play another World Series at Wrigley Field again. Sianis died in 1970 without lifting the curse. In 1969, 1984, 1989, and 2003, it looked as if the Cubs would break the Curse of the Billy Goat—only to fail each time.

It Really Happened

Charles "Gabby" Hartnett was a great power-hitting catcher during the 1920s and 1930s. He got his nickname because he talked a lot. He talked to batters while crouching behind the plate, he shouted encouragement to his teammates, and he also tried to distract Chicago's opponents with jokes and *insults*.

In the middle of the 1938 season, with the Cubs far out of first place, the team *promoted* the creaky-kneed catcher to manager. Hartnett was 37, and could only play two or three times a week. But he proved to be an excellent manager. That September, the Cubs went on an amazing streak. By September 28th, they *trailed* the first-place Pittsburgh Pirates by only one-half game.

That afternoon, the Cubs and Pirates played at Wrigley Field. The Pirates led 5–3 in the ninth inning, but the Cubs managed to tie the game. The skies were getting dark, and the fans wondered whether the umpires would allow the game to go on. The umps decided to play one more inning.

In the bottom of the tenth inning, Hartnett came to bat with two outs. He could barely see the baseball coming out of Mace Brown's hand. The Pittsburgh pitcher threw strike one past

Player-manager Gabby Hartnett watches the action from the Cubs' dugout.

Hartnett. He swung at the next pitch and barely fouled it off. On Brown's third pitch, Hartnett took a big cut and hit a long fly ball that disappeared into the darkness. No one could tell where the ball was going—except Hartnett. He knew he had hit a game-winning home run.

The 6–5 victory put the Cubs in first place. They never looked back, and won the pennant that year by two games. Hartnett's dramatic hit went down in history as the "Homer in the *Gloamin.*"

Team Spirit

The fans at Wrigley Field sit very close to players. It only makes sense that they feel close to the players, too. Cubs fans treat their players like family. If you do something to hurt the Cubs, you are the enemy. If an opposing player hits a home run—no matter how famous that player is—the fans at Wrigley will throw the ball back!

The fans sitting beyond the ivy-covered walls are the subject of the play *Bleacher Bums*, which has been performed for more than 30 years. The loudest bleacher bum may be Woo-Woo Wickers. He roams the stands yelling "Cubs Woo! Cubs Woo!"

Sometimes Cubs fans are more famous than the players. Regular visitors to Wrigley Field have included gangster Al Capone and actor Bill Murray. Hundreds of celebrities have sung *Take Me Out to the Ballgame* during the seventh-inning stretch. All Cubs fans are famous for one thing—they always believe that this year is "the year."

Cubs fans celebrate a victory outside of Wrigley Field.

Timeline

Frank
Chance

1874
The Cubs play their first season as the Chicago White Stockings.

1907
Frank Chance leads the Cubs to their first World Series championship.

1897
Cap Anson retires after 22 years in a Chicago uniform.

1932
The Cubs win their first of three pennants in the 1930s.

Cap
Anson

A special pin given to reporters at the 1932 World Series.

Phil
Cavarretta

Bruce
Sutter

1945
MVP Phil Cavarretta leads
the Cubs to the pennant.

1979
Bruce Sutter is just the second
reliever to win the **Cy Young Award**.

1959
Ernie Banks wins his
second MVP award.

2003
The Cubs come within
one victory of reaching
the World Series.

Ernie Banks

Fun Facts

WHALE OF A TALE

Wrigley Field, the home of the Cubs, was built for another team. The Chicago Whales of the **Federal League** were the first to use the park, in 1914.

A LEAGUE OF THEIR OWN

In 1943, team owner Philip Wrigley started the All-American Girls Professional Baseball League. It lasted 12 seasons, and was the subject of a hit movie in 1992.

GROUNDBREAKER

In 1962, the Cubs hired Buck O'Neil as a coach. He was the first African-American to hold a major-league coaching job.

LIGHTS OUT

Wrigley Field was the last ballpark to install lights for night baseball. The team actually bought light towers in the 1940s, but donated them to the Navy to help train sailors for World War II.

Ernie Banks meets young Cubs fans in Chicago.

LET'S PLAY TWO

Ernie Banks loved baseball so much that he was actually delighted to play doubleheaders. His favorite saying was "It's a great day for a ballgame—let's play two!"

A REAL VINE-TINGLER

Most Cubs love the famous ivy-covered walls of Wrigley Field. But not Lou Novikoff. He was the last person the Cubs should have put in the outfield. Novikoff had a medical condition that made every game torture—he had a fear of vines!

H.C. STORM SCHOOL

Talking Baseball

Ryne Sandberg

"Everything I am today…everything I have today…everything I will ever be… is because of the game of baseball."

—*Ryne Sandberg, on what baseball means to him*

"Defense is something I take pride in. I feel it's just as important as offense."

—*Derek Lee, on the importance of being an all-around player*

"Baseball gives a growing boy self-**poise** and **self-reliance**."

—*Al Spalding, on the sport as a character-builder*

"Baseball is too much of a sport to be a business, and too much of a business to be a sport."

—*Philip Wrigley, on owning a baseball team*

"The riches of the game are in the thrills, not the money."
— *Ernie Banks, on what was most important to him about baseball*

"I would tell my friends that I was going to be a big-league ballplayer and they would say, 'You're crazy. You're never going to amount to anything.'"
— *Sammy Sosa, on how baseball kept his dreams alive*

Sammy Sosa

For the Record

T he great Cubs teams and players have left their marks on the record books. These are the "best of the best"…

Ken Hubbs

Fergie Jenkins

CUBS AWARD WINNERS

WINNER	AWARD	YEAR
Rogers Hornsby	Most Valuable Player	1929
Gabby Hartnett	Most Valuable Player	1935
Phil Cavarretta	Most Valuable Player	1945
Hank Sauer	Most Valuable Player	1952
Ernie Banks	Most Valuable Player	1958
Ernie Banks	Most Valuable Player	1959
Billy Williams	Rookie of the Year	1961
Ken Hubbs	Rookie of the Year	1962
Fergie Jenkins	Cy Young Award *	1971
Bruce Sutter	Cy Young Award	1979
Rick Sutcliffe	Cy Young Award	1984
Ryne Sandberg	Most Valuable Player	1984
Jim Frey	Manager of the Year	1984
Andre Dawson	Most Valuable Player	1987
Jerome Walton	Rookie of the Year	1989
Don Zimmer	Manager of the Year	1989
Greg Maddux	Cy Young Award	1992
Kerry Wood	Rookie of the Year	1998
Sammy Sosa	Most Valuable Player	1998

The Cy Young award is given to the league's best pitcher each year.

CUBS ACHIEVEMENTS

ACHIEVEMENT	YEAR
N.L. Pennant Winners	1876
N.L. Pennant Winners	1880
N.L. Pennant Winners	1881
N.L. Pennant Winners	1882
N.L. Pennant Winners	1885
N.L. Pennant Winners	1886
N.L. Pennant Winners	1906
N.L. Pennant Winners	1907
World Series Champions	1907
N.L. Pennant Winners	1908
World Series Champions	1908
N.L. Pennant Winners	1910
N.L. Pennant Winners	1918
N.L. Pennant Winners	1929
N.L. Pennant Winners	1932
N.L. Pennant Winners	1935
N.L. Pennant Winners	1938
N.L. Pennant Winners	1945
N.L. East Champions	1984
N.L. East Champions	1989
N.L. Central Champions	2003

Ernie Banks accepts his 1959 N.L. MVP award.

Gabby Hartnett and Lon Warneke, stars of Chicago's pennant-winning teams of the 1930s.

Pinpoints

The history of a baseball team is made up of many smaller stories. These stories take place all over the map—not just in the city a team calls "home." Match the push-pins on these maps to the Team Facts and you will begin to see the story of the Cubs unfold!

TEAM FACTS

1   Chicago, Illinois—*The Cubs have played here since 1874.*

2   Marshalltown, Iowa—*Cap Anson was born here.*

3   Seattle, Washington—*Ron Santo was born here.*

4   Fresno, California—*Frank Chance was born here.*

5   Dallas, Texas—*Ernie Banks was born here.*

6   Whistler, Alabama—*Billy Williams was born here.*

7   Winston-Salem, North Carolina—*Mark Grace was born here.*

8   Lancaster, Pennsylvania—*Bruce Sutter was born here.*

9   Troy, New York—*Johnny Evers was born here.*

10   Chatham, Ontario (Canada)—*Fergie Jenkins was born here.*

11   San Pedro de Marcoris, Dominican Republic—*Sammy Sosa was born here.*

12   Puerto Cabella, Venezuela—*Carlos Zambrano was born here.*

Carlos Zambrano

Play Ball

Baseball is a game played between two teams over nine innings. Teams take one turn at bat and one turn in the field during each inning. A turn at bat ends when three outs are made. The batters on the hitting team try to reach base safely. The players on the fielding team try to prevent this from happening.

In baseball, the ball is controlled by the pitcher. The pitcher must throw the ball to the batter, who decides whether or not to swing at each pitch. If a batter swings and misses, it is a strike. If the batter lets a good pitch go by, it is also a strike. If the batter swings and the ball does not stay in fair territory (between the v-shaped lines that begin at home plate) it is called "foul," and is counted as a strike. If the pitcher throws three strikes, the batter is out. If the pitcher throws four bad pitches before that, the batter is awarded first base. This is called a base-on-balls, or "walk."

When the batter swings the bat and hits the ball, everyone springs into action. If a fielder catches a batted ball before it hits the ground, the batter is out. If a fielder scoops the ball off the ground and throws it to first base before the batter arrives, the batter is out. If the batter reaches first base safely, he is credited with a hit. A one-base hit is called a single, a two-base hit is called a double, a three-base hit is called a triple, and a four-base hit is called a home run.

Runners who reach base are only safe when they are touching one of the bases. If they are caught between the bases, the fielders can tag them with the ball and record an out.

A batter who is able to circle the bases and make it back to home plate before three outs are made is credited with a run scored. The team with the most runs after nine innings is the winner.

Anyone who has played baseball (or softball) knows that it can be a complicated game. Every player on the field has a job to do. Different players have different strengths and weaknesses. The pitchers, batters, and managers make hundreds of decisions every game. The more you play and watch baseball, the more "little things" you are likely to notice. The next time you are at a game, look for these plays:

PLAY LIST

DOUBLE PLAY—A play where the fielding team is able to make two outs on one batted ball. This usually happens when a runner is on first base, and the batter hits a ground ball to one of the infielders. The base runner is forced out at second base and the ball is then thrown to first base before the batter arrives.

HIT AND RUN—A play where the runner on first base sprints to second base while the pitcher is throwing the ball to the batter. When the second baseman or shortstop moves toward the base to wait for the catcher's throw, the batter tries to hit the ball to the place that the fielder has just left. If the batter swings and misses, the fielding team can tag the runner out.

INTENTIONAL WALK—A play when the pitcher throws four bad pitches on purpose, allowing the batter to walk to first base. This happens when the pitcher would much rather face the next batter—and is willing to risk putting a runner on base.

SACRIFICE BUNT—A play where the batter makes an out on purpose so that a teammate can move to the next base. On a bunt, the batter tries to "deaden" the pitch with the bat instead of swinging at it.

SHOESTRING CATCH—A play where an outfielder catches a short hit an inch or two above the ground, near the tops of his shoes. It is not easy to run as fast as you can and lower your glove without slowing down. It can be risky, too. If a fielder misses a shoestring catch, the ball might roll all the way to the fence.

Glossary

BASEBALL WORDS TO KNOW

ALL-AROUND—Good at all parts of the game.

ALL-STAR—A player who is selected to play in baseball's annual All-Star Game.

BLEACHER SEATS—The unprotected seats located in the outfield, where fans get "bleached" by the sun.

CY YOUNG AWARD—The trophy given to the league's best pitcher each year.

DOUBLEHEADER—Two games scheduled to be played in one day.

DRAFT—The meeting at which teams take turns choosing the best amateur players each year.

FEDERAL LEAGUE—A third major league that played two seasons, 1914 and 1915.

FORCE-OUT—An out made by touching a base that a runner is forced to run to.

GRANDSTAND—The section of seats that makes up the tall (or "grand") part of a ball park.

HALL OF FAME—The museum in Cooperstown, NY where baseball's greatest players are honored. A player voted into the Hall of Fame is sometimes called a "Hall of Famer."

LEADOFF HITTER—The first hitter in a lineup, or the first hitter in an inning.

MAJOR LEAGUES—The top level of professional baseball leagues. The American League (A.L.) and National League (N.L.) make up today's major leagues. Sometimes called the "big leagues."

MINOR LEAGUES—The many professional leagues that help develop players for the major leagues.

MOST VALUABLE PLAYER (MVP)—An award given each year to the league's top player; an MVP is also selected for the World Series and All-Star Game.

NATIONAL LEAGUE (N.L.)—The older of the two major leagues; the N.L. began play in 1876 and the American League (A.L.) started in 1901.

PENNANT—A league championship. The term comes from the triangular flag awarded to each season's champion, beginning in the 1870s.

POSTSEASON—The games played after the regular season, including the playoffs and World Series.

RELIEF—The role of substitute pitcher, or "reliever."

ROOKIE OF THE YEAR—An annual award given to each league's best first-year player.

RUNS BATTED IN (RBIs)—A statistic that counts the number of runners a batter drives home.

SLIDER—A fast pitch that curves and drops just as it reaches the batter.

STRUCK OUT THE SIDE—Retired all three batters in the same inning on strikes.

WORLD SERIES—The world championship series played between the winners of the National League and American League.

OTHER WORDS TO KNOW

EARNEST—Serious and dedicated.

EVAPORATE—Disappear, or turn into a vapor.

FIERY—With strong feeling.

FLANNEL—A soft wool or cotton material.

GLOAMIN—A poetic word meaning twilight.

IDENTICAL—The same.

INSULTS—Words meant to hurt someone's feelings.

LOGO—A symbol or design that represents a company or team.

MANGLED—Cut and crushed.

POISE—Calm and confidence.

PROMOTED—Gave a better job.

QUAINT—Cute and old-fashioned.

SELF-RELIANCE—The ability to depend on oneself.

SOUVENIR—Something kept as a reminder of a place or event.

SYNTHETIC—Made in a laboratory, not in nature.

TRAILED—Was behind.

TAVERN— A place that serves food and drinks.

TRADITION—A belief or custom that is handed down from generation to generation.

Places to Go

ON THE ROAD

WRIGLEY FIELD
1060 West Addison Street
Chicago, Illinois 60613
(773) 404-2827

NATIONAL BASEBALL HALL OF FAME AND MUSEUM
25 Main Street
Cooperstown, New York 13326
(888) 425-5633
www.baseballhalloffame.org

ON THE WEB

THE CHICAGO CUBS   www.Cubs.com
 * *to learn more about the Cubs*

MAJOR LEAGUE BASEBALL   www.mlb.com
 * *to learn about all the major league teams*

MINOR LEAGUE BASEBALL   www.minorleaguebaseball.com
 * *to learn more about the minor leagues*

ON THE BOOKSHELVES

To learn more about the sport of baseball, look for these books at your library or bookstore:

 * January, Brendan. *A Baseball All-Star*. Chicago, IL.: Heinemann Library, 2005.
 * Kelly, James. *Baseball*. New York, NY.: DK, 2005.
 * Mintzer, Rich. *The Everything Kids' Baseball Book*. Cincinnati, OH.: Adams Media Corporation, 2004.

Index

PAGE NUMBERS IN **BOLD** REFER TO ILLUSTRATIONS.

The Team

MARK STEWART has written more than 25 books on baseball, and over 100 sports books for kids. He grew up in New York City during the 1960s rooting for the Yankees and Mets, and now takes his two daughters, Mariah and Rachel, to the same ballparks. Mark comes from a family of writers. His grandfather was Sunday Editor of The *New York Times* and his mother was Articles Editor of *Ladies Home Journal* and *McCall's*. Mark has profiled hundreds of athletes over the last 20 years. He has also written several books about his native New York and New Jersey, his home today. Mark is a graduate of Duke University, with a degree in history. He lives with his daughters and wife, Sarah, overlooking Sandy Hook, NJ.

JAMES L. GATES, JR. has served as Library Director at the National Baseball Hall of Fame since 1995. He had previously served in academic libraries for almost fifteen years. He holds degrees from Belmont Abbey College, the University of Notre Dame and Indiana University. During his career Jim has authored several academic articles and has served in an editorial capacity on multiple book, magazine and museum publications, and he also serves as host for the Annual Cooperstown Symposium on Baseball and American Culture. He is an ardent Baltimore Orioles fan and enjoys watching baseball with his wife and two children.